AF421701

I fear my fatal flaw is to speak.
once I begin, I cannot stop;
a flow of delicate idiocies
illegible to all who aren't me.
transcribe my mind
and teach me how to cope in ways that aren't
grass and other blades or
relying on others to heal.
swallow me whole
and tell me I'm not
plagued by the beautifully curated;
convince me it isn't true that
all this time, I have been my mother's daughter.

ten fingers too many

art&design by Lauren Wander
poetry by Lauren Wander

poetry for both the *lover* and the *fighter*
who live in us all.

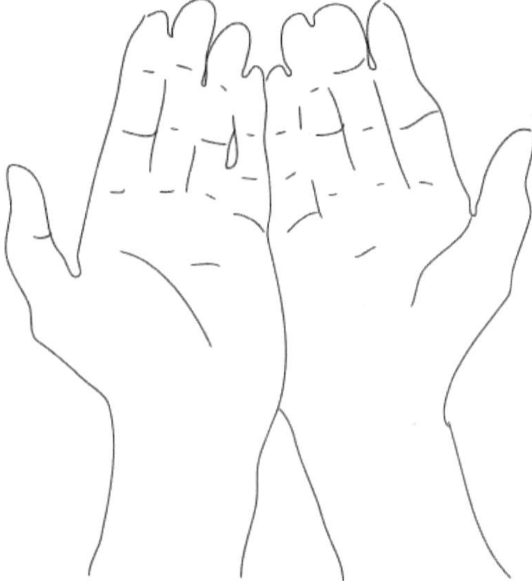

foreword

disclaimer– the author of this work states, though loosely based on herself, parts may be fictitious; any resemblance to actual persons, living or dead, or actual events is purely coincidental.

Poetry may involve strong language which may not be suitable for young readers. Mental illness, health struggles, and addiction are often glamorized in books, films, and on social media. The aim of this poetry collection is not to do so; rather, quite the opposite. Mental illness should neither be stigmatized nor romanticized. Always reach out for help if and when you need it. *mental health emergency hotline– 988*

ten fingers too many *by Lauren Wander*

I. swallow me whole

II. mother's daughter

III. my fatal flaw

IV. grass and other blades

V. transcribe my mind

I.

swallow me whole

Promise me

That my sharp skeleton hasn't

Pricked your finger in a way unforgivable;

That the stitches holding us together

Aren't snagging; that

Lacing my fingers through yours hasn't

Irrevocably damaged the landscape

Of your hand; and

To be alone with me won't end in

Suffocation; toxicity.

Promise me.

Even if it means you have to lie.

I have scooped out my soft innards and juiced them on these pages; so when you taste, please tell me it is sweet but not too sweet; and maybe, just maybe you'll take another sip.

oh, my love, I promise.
I am so very good at
pretending.

...

A lack of indulgence;
An insensitivity to the beautiful;
Is sin as much as gluttony.
Earth exists abundantly
For the grasp of humans.
I am full up; filled to the brim.
I am filled with love for
Humankind: friend & stranger.
I am filled with beautiful prose
Dedicated to the world around me.
If only you could examine
My mind; for sometimes I cannot
Find delicate enough words and
These truths go unspoken.

Friendship is a type of romance.
I have felt some of the most
Fascination; connection; allure;
In moments of female friendship.

In my head, these memories replay
Each frame overlaid with pink satin;
The edges curling from the humidity
Of palms aching to hold on a bit longer

To nights when I first told truths with
That little girl I learned to trust while
We danced; uncoordinated; off-beat.
In those moments, I learned vulnerability.

I have felt nothing short of love
In conversation; accompaniment.
Romance isn't merely erotic, but
Beautifully, platonically, fulfilling.

I dug a deep hole just to prove I could crawl out and
Became something I hated just to understand why.
You chase the dwindling burnt end of a cigarette
Like it's the person you've always been, but I know.
I remember late nights, early mornings, talks of
What we could be, oh such endless opportunity.
When you failed to follow and stayed with the worms,
You decided getting worse was the easiest way out.
Though I've got dirt under my nails, at least it's over.
But I cannot dig you out of your own hole, and
I cannot crawl for you, my broken marionette.
To stay down too long is to rot; become worm food.
Sometimes I still try and yell for you, but they've
Packed your ears with dirt and your mouth with lies.
My stomach is too soft to stand by and just watch.
I'm far too squeamish to stay as you decompose.
Though I know you think you've found Wonderland,
The worms just want your body, not your person.
Not friend, just food. But you must know that by now.

I wish you would hug me
but I'm afraid of what you may feel
through the fabric of my shirt

Though my graveyard is in the sun,
It still contains the dead; and
Though it may be picturesque,
Digging six feet down reveals truth.
In a trance-like, catatonic waltz,
I make; pluck my way through a
Monument of tombs and souls;
Lovers; thinkers. Beatless hearts.
Put your ear to the Earth and
You may still hear them rambling.
A quiet pain; A confusing lonely;
Considering so many lay here.

In the car with my mom once,
I accidentally said I was 16.
When I got home I cried
Wet tears on my dry pillow;
Took one thing and made
It something else, completely;
Wound the clock back and
Believed it actually worked.
How is it I always manage
To crave what once was,
But what once was only
Exists when it has passed?
One day you'll wake and you're
18 and things have changed,
And you're still young
But you're, oh, so old.
You will try anything to feel the
Yank of the present moment;
Splash cold water on your
Warm face, time and time again,
Until you finally forget how

Time feels like a gut punch when you're young.

Look at me!
I yelled.
I am here!
I am now!
I am never again!
I exist!
Look at me!

I read Plato, Marcus Aurelius, and Socrates;
I only understood the half of it, though I plead.
I watched as man underestimated what's at stake
And I swore not to make the same mistake.
I chewed and digested and wanted to believe
I swear, I heard what they taught me and I see
The line of reason drawn from here to there,
Yet unknowingly, I trudge my own path elsewhere.
I wish I could believe the soul's immortality
Or all the things I have the chance to be;
I've tried stoicism; nihilism; another's creation,
Unraveling myself to avoid damnation.
Yet none of them fit my long limbs and extremities
And it's not like I believe in half the entities
In my modern renaissance, I'll learn from the past
To create something in me that'll truly last.
I've found simplicity through inspiration
But I refuse to become their recreation;
I read history to influence not harness,
And it helped me create a religion in purpose.

Let me run my finger down
The curve of your nose and
The silhouette of your cheek

For I could draw all day but
When pencil meets paper, it's
Always your face that emerges.

I will chip away pieces from
This block of marble to reveal,
with unblinking eyes, your unseen

So maybe one day I could
Memorize every angle; contour;
Like an Athenian Greek god.

I have not yet learned to capture
One's undying generosity and
Unabashed love like something

Sculpted; carved of stone, but
Even in blindness, even in death;
I may never, will never, forget.

Cook a warm meal with the one you love. Pay attention when they tell you about their day. Be honest with them when they ask how you're doing. Sit together and eat. Enjoy your food. Enjoy your company. And here, in this simplicity, lies the meaning of it all.

I do not run because I like it.
I run to feel; to clear my head.

This raised heart rate serves to
Imitate something I am not allowed;

Injecting veins with false adrenaline
To satiate a hunger for what was

Unknown only until I bathed in
Newfound understanding; purpose.

Without the fingers of my lover
Laced through mine, it is these

Short-term regulations I chase
To feel something so strong;

When I am condemned to
Live a moment without you.

Holding water is an impossibility;
Slipping between the cracks;
Running down forearms like
Fruit juice while a child devours;
Do not hold, do not wait;
Drink me down.

I want to live deep;
Anything but obsolete.
I crave true sensation;
To create my narration.
Six feet down isn't deep
Enough for me to sleep;
So I must graze bedrock
To hear fulfillment's knock.
Must I breach insane
Simply just to obtain
What I so direly need;
For what I require, I plead.
I was prescribed life
Beyond endless strife.

Even when the world or the people in it
Feel like they are all working against you,
An eternal yet pointless charade of us & them,
Something to be pressed firmly against,
Remember that your life is yours only
And if the Earth isn't for living in and
Experiencing in, then what is it even for?
Remember that this world is here for you and
It isn't against *you*; *you're* against *yourself*.
Life shouldn't be something to be stretched
Until it nearly bursts; seams popping
Ominously as you trudge along; evermore.
It has been elastic all along and this
Constriction is but a figment of your imagination.
You have to let yourself do what you want
For the first time in your life, even if it means
Taking chances; disappointing some.
Suddenly you'll notice the world just wants
You to succeed; to choose to live for yourself;
And the people who really love you will
Want nothing more than to help you do so.

Lauren Wander

May I occupy a corner
Of your lovely mind like a
chair tucked under a desk
Or a fly on the wall;

You don't even have to
Notice I'm there, just
Let me live in your
Immortal subconscious.

Flick a coin in a wishing well just
To see the water ripple upon impact.
Search for meaning and perspective
In the clear reflection now disrupted.

Nobody really cares, I should give up.
Nobody really cares, I am free to be.

My future is unclear, I am directionless.
My future is unclear, I could do anything.

I feel things deeply, I'm far too emotional.
I feel things deeply, I appreciate everything.

I've changed, I'll never be that girl again.
I've changed, I love who I'm becoming.

The looking glass has cleared right
As the clock strikes midnight and a
New self emerges from the shimmering
Pool with ripples now slowly stilling.

I am plagued by the beautifully curated;
and I want nothing more than for it to
swallow me whole, lick its fingers, and

never apologize.

never apologize. never apologize. never apologize.

II.

mother's daughter

But when promises break,
I am afraid of this face;
Inescapably leering in
Every reflective surface.
There is fear behind going,
But even more behind not.
To avoid inevitable mistakes
Is to avoid the possibility of
Prosperity; success; rebirth.
What will become of me?
I stop myself before I have
The chance to prove myself;
And my biggest fear is that
Nobody will ever get to see
The person I could be.

I
don't
want
to
fight.

I
hate
realizing
that
you're
right

and
I
just
don't
want

to
admit
that
I'm
wrong.

you
could
do
so
much
better.

and
what
worries
me
is

one
day
you
will
realize.

I will have my cake, and
I'm going to eat it too.
Bite by bite, consuming
Thick, dense calories.
I will swallow; acceptance.
But like every single time,
It'll get stuck in my throat
And I'll have to throw it up.
Oh; the rejection of self.
I didn't deserve it anyway.

girlhood
is pulchritudinous; painfully beautiful.
I may be suffering; I may be in pain;
but do you find me captivating; alluring?
say you do, for
the only antidote I need
is your word.

Borrowed eyes from my mother;
Walk a mile in the shoes of my father.
Roped ladders of genetic code;
Curated; exemplary; faultless.
But like ink stains on a white page;
The answer to a question you
Knew I would never understand;
There is a part of me that exists like
Carvings in bone; my mind's eye;
Crafted with nobody to blame but me.
It is my *faultfaultfaultfaultfault.*
From where did it come? Why?
Oh; breath in my lungs,
Exhale how you have wronged me.
Set me back at the beginning;
Make me what they thought
They were getting until I became
Me. And everything went wrong.

I can only be seen if I am perfect. I
can only be seen if I am perfec
t. I can only be seen if I am p
erfect. I can only be seen if
I am perfect. I can only
be seen if I am p
erfect. I c
an
only b
e seen if I
am perfect. I can
only be seen if I am per
fect. I can only be seen if I a
m perfect. I can only be seen if
I am perfect. I can only be seen
if I am perfect. I can only be seen if-

Oh, how I wish I could change.
Not be such a burden to the
People who just want to love me.
Learn to understand myself so
I'm easier to accept; put up with.
It shouldn't be walking on eggshells;
Avoiding hairline cracks; just
In order to spend time with me.
Alas, I hold my loved ones to a
Standard of perfection I don't meet.
I long to be less obsessive; neurotic.
Write a better song with better lyrics.
To refuse what I don't want
And learn to accept what I do.
They say life is mine for the taking;
Glue together your pieces; change.
But I've already touched it,
And it is already tainted; so
I'll probably just stay the same.

My biggest desire is to be alone so I do not
Disturb; perturb anyone else with my presence.
At least when I am alone, nobody has to
Be afraid of me. I do not have to fear the pressure
Of being seen; mortifying ordeal of being known.
But like salt in the wound; twisting the knife;
To be alone is almost worse. For now, I have
Nobody to hide behind; and I must face the
Animal all alone; unveiling my truth, indefinitely.

I want to peel my skin off.
Take a step outside of my body
And finally see what everyone else does.
When the problem is bone-deep,
We place blame on the skin because
It's the easiest to restore; regulate.
I want to run and never stop.
Do something rash and feel the repercussions.
Finally revel in the burning in my lungs
That means I'm really, truly alive.
When will I finally be content?
Oh; obsessive, perfectionistic me.
No matter how much I reprimand the skin,
It still surrounds me. And I know I cannot,
And will not ever, compare.

My siren song rings
Lies and deceit.
Plug your ears with wax
And leave while you can.
Can't you hear me?
I am abrasive.
I am manipulative.
You shouldn't have to
Tie yourself down
So I won't hurt you.
Let me warn you:
It's all my fault.
Let me watch from
A distance; protect you;
So I can't break the one
Good thing I finally had.

The Acceptance

I was never good at speaking in front of crowds, but I guess today is the day I don't really have a choice.

Ehem.
First of all, and most importantly, I'd like to thank you all for being here. I can't think of better people with whom to spend my acceptance; the acceptance of something so detrimental and important to my future. I'd like to thank everyone, from the bottom of my heart.

Can I say a few quick words?
Alright. A couple minutes.

The hardest concept I've had to wrap my head around on this journey is the fragility of life. Danger, insecurity, and fear are imminent nearly one hundred percent of the time. I do not need to be living dangerously to be living freely. As a human, I am delicate. I have begun to learn just how fast the unthinkable really can happen; does happen. Protect yourself. You are your top priority.

My view of the world, in the past, was flawed. I do not know all of the answers. Embarrassment and mistakes are inescapable. We all die. Those who outlive us will find ways to keep living. The time you spend here probably won't be significant to the general population, but that doesn't mean it isn't significant to some. And that is truly all that matters.

This acceptance is the most difficult thing I think I will ever have to do, and not only because of the massive crowd in front of me. To be watched, seen, heard, and believed is difficult and scary, yet not as scary as finally coming to terms with the inescapable aspects of life. I truly am glad you are all here to witness this acceptance, a step in the right direction toward a fruitful life that has only just begun.

Thank you.

the less you speak,

the more they listen.

I applaud my body,

For within her dwells the
True specter. Maturity means
Acceptance; and after
Berating her performance;
Slitting her costume to
Unspool her rotten guts;
My body deserves an
Overdue standing ovation.
My heart continues its
Stubborn beat and my
Thoughts stay just sharp
Enough to discern that
My body bears the brunt, but
My mind is the antagonist; so

I applaud my body.

Use and reuse me.
Recycle and reshape.
I've fit so many molds
I cannot seem to; begin to;
Remember my original form.
It must've been hideous, for
When I saw the opportunity
To change, I seized it
Before I fully realized the
Impacts; repercussions.
Fingerprints wiped away and
Towels left to dry on the line.
May that very breeze carry me
Somewhere far away where
Somebody else may have the
Chance to use and reuse me.
Recycle and reshape.

I wake before the rest, yet still,
by night, they beat me to sleep.

I grind my teeth until fangs become nubs
and will still never be satiated like the rest, I
~~chew swallow chew swallow chew swallow~~
and still—

I wake before the rest.

III.

my fatal flaw

I feel as though my Achilles' heel is the ability to see clearly; those who see clearest suffer most. For we; humankind; are not faultless. It is just a certain blurriness of vision that allows for an uninterrupted blissful dance through life by those who were blessed by fallible sight.

Follow the rabbit
Follow the rabbit
Follow the rabbit
Until you remember
Never not doing so
And this is your new
World; your new life.

Down

Down

Down

Until you can see nothing
But *therabbittherabbittherabbit*
And you are no longer
Moving toward a destination
But just for the sake of
Moving; *goinggoinggoing*.
Fake progression just
To prove you are trying.

Two sides of my mind fight for
Bodily autonomy; control; willpower.
Though driving with the windows
Down only tangles my hair,
When the weather is just right
And the air is golden, insatiable
Urges tell me open windows
Are necessary. *Be loud; scream!*
But remorse screams louder.
Is opening up; catharsis; the key?
Or is this just another self-sabotage?

control. willpower. control. willpower. control. willpower.

Though I like to pretend that I know,
I'm really just a kid. My surroundings
Are changing so fast I'm motion sick.
If I could stop the train, I'd jump off
Where I could crawl back inside the
Comfortable, dark womb of my mother.
Back where I was still a blank slate
Without fear of irreparable damage.

I am afraid my fatal flaw is to speak;
and once I begin, the words will

      never

          stop

              flowing.

When my hair reaches past my shoulders,
Everything will fall into place the way nature
Intended it to be; before I became what I am
And what I will always be. I can poke and prod;
Convince myself hard enough that I can change,
But in six month's time it's always the same.
I return back to the place from which I came;
I have found my other and destroyed her, and
I am with no differences visible to the naked eye.

I am smooth; I am docile.
I am the curtains with a breeze in them. Move me; pose me however you want. I am the sand falling down an hourglass; put in her place; inevitably. I was probably wrong. I'll do better. No, it's my fault. Don't worry. I'm sorry. Please let me try again. What works best for you? Don't worry about me; I'll adapt. Make me your girl; your bitch. I am resilient. I am easy. I don't have any complaints. I'll take your hits; no resistance.
I am smooth; I am docile.

and I will continue to regret it.

every.single.time.

What I need is
For you to be happy.
To know I have
Pleased others
Will please me
More than any
other
Option for my
sake.
I have spent so long
Making sure everyone
else is accommodated
for I don't even know
What I need anymore.
What do I want?
What do I enjoy?
Whatever you want.
Will you tell me,
Please? So I know
What to do?

To feel empathy is to ache; endure.

To watch somebody you love suffer
Is to suffer yourself. To find yourself

At a draw; all your chips bet; wasted
Odds; chances; opportunities. Craving

Nothing but to cease the misery; pain;
Of the one you care for. Yet; still no

Winning hand in the ceaseless game.

Today I will wash the dishes and do
What I've been putting off for so long.
My negligence has grown legs and
Become something I fear I cannot tame.
Day-old coffee; scalded milk; becoming
Evil, like spilled blood; a headless figure.
I am the type to keep feeding the beast
Even though it's terrifyingly overgrown;
Putting priority on *it* instead of *me*.
My pile of dishes has grown a mouth.
It tells me now, there is no use; too late.
For when I lose control, neglect ensues, and
Care for my surroundings is the first to go.
Once the pile begins, I may as well add.
What was once now's responsibility
Pushed to a future version of myself.
She has initiative; motivation; ambition.
If I could just kill the beast, I could
Finally be that girl: cleaned and pressed.
Today I will wash the dishes so that
Tomorrow I may be brand new once more
And be free to finally do everything else
I've been neglecting to satiate the beast.

maybe,

all

along,

the

problem

really

was

just

me.

wash out my mouth with soap and remind me
that I am the problem.
wash out my mouth with soap
and remind me that I am
the problem. wash out my
mouth with soap and remind me that I

Lauren Wander

I live in a glass castle;
My unconvincingly camouflaged
Place on stage; forever seen
With an unwavering eye constantly
And perpetually on me; Cuts;
Bruises don't go unnoticed when
Big Brother is watching; waiting
For the crowd the form; tap the glass;
Press their ugly noses to the window
Between my world and theirs.

to be everybody's is to be nobody's.
I want to be somebody's.

You've been treated unfairly and left
On patches of Earth deemed unlivable.
You've been fooled into believing one thing and
Begrudgingly forced yourself into realizing the truth.
You've been deceived before; you remember
The bone-deep; guttural pain of duplicity.
What compels one to sustain; foster; nurture
A relationship for so long only to suddenly
Kick the other to the curb, leave them in the dirt?
To take that desolate land and transform it;
A metamorphosis; into something fruitful
Is the most self-serving yet respectful way
To grow from this certain type of demise.
Grow from the dirt that they left you in.
Now, your tree grows in the corner of a forest;
Untouched by others and not seen by most.
If a tree falls with nobody to hear it,
Does it still make a sound? Heal yourself.
In the presence of nobody else, take this time
To finally *grow from the dirt that they left you in.*

IV.

grass and other blades

Oh; but when I die, may I
Occupy a beautiful grave;
With a beautiful tombstone?
May they remember me
As a girl; unafraid; true.
An artist; thinker; poet.
Remind them how I loved
Deeply and assured.
I was a sister and daughter.
I was an admirer. Please;
Don't let them forget.
For, one day, mine will
Just be another beautiful
Grave; tombstone; among
The others, yearning
To be remembered.

I wish that to know me wasn't to hurt.

My knives-out, bleeding-heart combination.
It's more than satire and irony; confusion
Akin to the likes of cognitive dissonance.
To know my good is to have survived my bad;
And I want to be remembered but not known.
Hold me close and lie that I am fragile, though

I am jagged, frightening, and rough.
I am difficult to be around; stop lying.
You don't have to try and convince me.
I throw blame because it's what I know.
I wrote the script and watched you read it;
I pretended I didn't know how it would end

But I am sick of pretending.

please let me go.

I can see the light
and the grass is so soft.
the bugs never bite
and I can run for so long;

one sting kills; like a bee
harming no one else.
they are safe, far from me
inviting them to hell's

great immortal show.

Maybe if I just tried harder.
Do I have enough energy
To try just one more time?
I think I could muster it up.
Maybe I could try to change.
If it means you will stop
Having to worry, I can
Keep pretending to be ok.
I can take a little bit more.
Look how much better
I've gotten, already; see how
Hard I am trying for you?
I will leave my room to feel
The rejuvenation of the sun and
Convince myself *"it's going
To really work this time, I swear."*
And yes, I know I'm not perfect
Because I am not yet getting
Better for me, but for you.
I'm working on it, I promise.
I'll work on it. *For you.*

Lauren Wander

Grounding myself by
Standing on raw Earth
Barefooted; barehearted;
Imagining the growth
Of roots from each toe.
Earth's fine delicacies,
Only taken advantage of
By some, never cease
To put me back in my
Rightful place: just human.
No more; no less.
Let this be a comfort.

Sometimes,
it's fun to let it all catch up
with me. A game of cat and
mouse; how long can I run? I'll let
you pull me down into your hole
with you and pour the antidote down
my throat; pretend I'm that old version
of myself with thoughts like molasses and honey: anything sickly
sweet. How easy it would be to slip back
into that old place; almost as if I'd
never even left. No wonder you
stayed; oh so sweet until
it's sour.

like pitted cherries or spilled wine,
I'm a sad excuse for the abundance
of what once could've been.

Tying ribbons in hair is simply
Distraction from the veneer
Shaped to perfectly adhere to
A room of imperfect faces.
Though we frolic in fields
By day, we sleepwalk in them
By night; lapsed when we wake.
I am strong because I am human.
I am human because I am strong.
May I have the courage to go on
So inconspicuous like the rest;
Those whom I've come to detest;
As individuality is suicide.

I'm done putting it off.
I'm done making excuses.
I'm done letting others
Take their turn before mine.

It

is

my

turn.

It is my turn to resurrect.

In church, I was taught
From dust we began and
To dust we shall return.
In church, I prayed on my
Knees until the skin tore
To bone and still; God
Never answered. Is it
Absurd to buy every flower
Just to place them back where
They came from? Tell me,
God, why do some people
Take and never give back?
If we will return to which
We came, in the end,
Why place such pride in
Physical possession? Put back
What was never yours and
Take lessons from those hours
Spent praying on your knees;
For everything that once was
Will always be; to dust.

I dream of one day
growing roots but
the wind still carries me,
carelessly, day by day.

I would like to allow myself to
Live life intensely; feel intensely;
Let the rain pour when it may.
Find romance in the mundane, like
A mother's bond with a child, or
Cafuné– caressing a lover's hair.
Mother nature unapologetically
Brings storms, and so might I.
Though I may hide behind a
Convincing assuredness, I am
A master of camouflage; mendacity.
I would like to allow myself to
Live life intensely; feel intensely;
Let the rain pour when it may.
But oh; how I am afraid.

It is vital to leave your detention and feel
A sun-warmed face; grass between toes.
Learn from those other living things you
May stumble upon on your journey; they're
More similar to us than we may imagine.
We may be humans, but we are still animals.

Leave your fingerprints on something other than
Your water-damaged diary; that one stuffed animal.
Notice the way the pink turns to purple and blue
When the sky is no longer crying but the sun is
Setting; waving goodbye with the promise that
It'll be back tomorrow and every day after.

dandelion fluff floating freely through
summer air thick with fever;
perpetually searching for home and never
finding solace. dandelion fluff floating freely
through summer air thick with fever; perpetually searching
for home and never finding solace.
dandelion fluff floating
freely through summer air thick
with fever; perpetually searching for home
and never finding solace.

I have spent so many years searching.
May I finally find what I have been looking for.

I am not good with
Something so fragile as

Love.

I am too clumsy.
My claws; my teeth
Are much too sharp.
You are not safe; yet
Somehow you trust
Your heart in my hands.
I don't know how you
Could ever see me as

Good;

But I am trying.
I am trying to be good.
I am trying for you.

Oh; how am I to spend
The rest of my meandering life?
I'm too young to be a cynic.
I can already see through
The cracks we, as humans,
Try so desperately to patch.
But with something so fragile,
Cracks should be expected.
I wasn't born seeing the use in
Fixing something already so broken;
Why repair cracks that will
Just return with a vengeance?
Others may see the cracks but
They don't let it define their world.
Yet day in; day out; I wonder:
How will I waste so much time?
Will I continue to perform,
Perpetually masked, like
I always have; always will?
It doesn't matter, really.
> **-The time will pass anyway.**

It won't take a day.
Or a week. Or a month.
This dog keeps on running
Whether I follow or not.
My heels have blisters and
My mind works against me.
Each second is anguish,
And my fingers slip; sweaty.
Days pass just the same
If I do or don't comply.
The time will pass anyway
So I might as well try.

the space between each of my vertebrae expands
as I stretch higher on my toes, reaching for
the highest peach on the tallest tree.
let it be mine without struggle.

I sat and I waited and I watched and
I listened and I stayed patient; and still
Nothing happened. I do not know what
I see when I am entranced. I do not know
What I am thinking; perhaps nothing at all.
A dead girl walking; the closest I will ever
Be to death before I really see the light.
I wanted so much from life. I wanted to *work*
And to *move* and to *live* and to *go go go*.
Alas, I did not pick the right path, I fear,
For I sat and I waited and I watched and
I listened and I stayed patient; yet still,

I never *lived*.

V.

transcribe my mind

please

ah, that horrible comfort of

succumbing to what you know best.

       back

   back

back

to the beginning.

Jealousy is a faultline I walk, careless
Of the quakes it sends in my wake.
Why must I assume the worst in people,
Especially those who have never
Done something to raise my suspicion?
I have a fear of abandonment, and I am
Searching for signs of it as if it's what I want.
I fear my grip is too tight, I have no
Choice but to puncture who I love.
I cannot ask for help because I can
See that the problem is me, yet I find myself
A maze of unfixable trials; never-ending.
Why can nobody seem to understand
That hyper-awareness is my issue?
It is what I am always so praised for.
Can't you see how it's making me
Crazy to know what's really wrong?
Yet with each passing day, the silence gets
Easier, and my mouth grows thick with it.

I must remind myself
Stubbornly; repeatedly;

Again and again; that
Just because I was treated

A certain way in the past
Does not mean history

Is condemned to repeat.
Good is out there, and

This I know because
It manifests itself in you.

Girls make dying beautifully lustworthy.
They make it something to crave.
Covered in satin; sprayed with perfume.
You want to be just like her, right?
As long as she carefully preserves
The outside; the shell; the beautiful facade;
No one will have to see what it's hiding.
No one will ever know she is rotting
Until the decay reaches the surface.
And no matter how hard they try, by then
She is too far gone to be saved.
The hyenas have sniffed out her
Decomposing lies. They know that scent;
Dying. And to them, dead is dead.
Nothing more; nothing beautiful. Dead.

Lauren Wander

to
what
extent
will
we
still
let
the
ends
justify
the
means?

the ends ~~justify the~~ means

justify? how does one justify?

I am instability and
Self-consciousness.

I am the last vulture
Only picking meat
Off bone when they've
Seen it done first.

I am lying through
Teeth, crooked and
Imperfect, about who
I am not; wish I was.

I am bitten cuticles,
Chipped nail polish,
Thinning hair, and
Piled, dirty dishes.

I am picking at skin
Though I know it
Only makes the
Problem worse.

I am seething jealousy;
I am guilty eyes, blaming
You for what only I
Have done to myself.

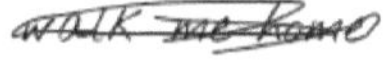

I would rather stumble
Home alone in the dark than
Inconvenience another with
The burden of my company.
I am directionless; I am tired.
I am dangerously close to
Catching fire; letting it burn.
Unapologetically burning out.
Every day feels like television
Static layered on white noise
Layered on an old silent film.
I do not have the energy to
Stop being the antagonist.
I *lie lie lie again again again*
Because I do not want help;
I am self-sufficient. *Another lie.*
Inconvenience; directionless; tired.
Tell me where to go; tell me how
You view me; tell me to my face
Before the flames burn out.
You know me better than I do.

I'll say
I'm happy where I am.
which I will insist
over and over
because I do not have the strength to go on.

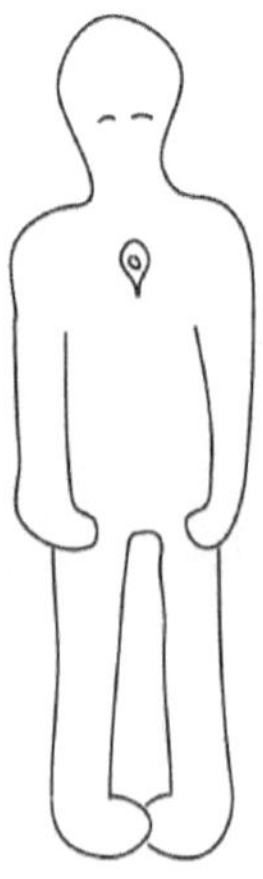

I am nothing if not the
Reason for bruised fruit.
Remind me that squeezing;

Holding tight with fear
Will indent the baby-smooth
Surface when I finally let go.

Impossible to wipe away, for
Bruises reach much too deep.
I am wanted until I am not.

I am walking secondhand-embarrassment.
My friends are the loveliest of lovely people.
If I were them, I couldn't stand to be around me.
They've seen me cry; they were there when
Everybody else left the party. They stayed
When others would've gone and weren't scared
When I yelled what should've been unforgivable.
We go out for coffee like nothing ever happened.
They give me book recommendations while
Somehow looking past the slew of irreversible,
Angry, black sludge that left my mouth that night.
My subconscious can't help but remind me
There is, there must be, something wrong.
Maybe there is something off in the way
They are too quick to forgive. Let me remind you
There is something intrinsically wrong with me;
Can't you see it? It's threatening to bubble over.
You should run now; I wouldn't blame you.
I have never heard anything to confirm my
Suspicions, but I am sure. My mind is made up.
I cannot be swayed. The shower walls stay
Webbed with hair; the floor littered with
Chewed nails; a sort of reprimanding myself.
But I cannot change. So I will try and present
My most bearable sides in order to keep the
People in my life who I do not deserve anyway.

Such a rash decision.
Was it the right decision?
It seems I did not plan
And now here I am
Stomping on thin ice
Like it'll never break.
Here on stage, I wonder
Which came first,
The bow or the applause?
Blink and you miss it.
Finally my turn; yet
When I recall, the applause
Had only started once I
Had already begun bowing.

who should I be

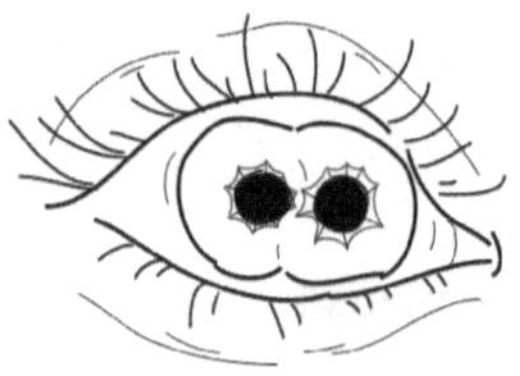

today?

look how i have improved!

97

i went outside and

my skin sizzled like bacon and i was the prized ham

and i smiled but i also lied

and fat dripped off of me in gobs of deceit

and broken promises of the bettering

that would never happen.

Like a crazed Victorian woman prescribed a visit to the sea to clear her psychotic mind, I am set free by nature. When your thoughts cannot be transcribed, and you cannot lay out a map of your mind, they cannot truly understand what you need; so they send you away. The sea is not the cure, though it does set fire to my mind; it is not what I need, but its repercussions are. I am to stay away from society for just long enough to begin again and them to bring me back home; all better.

these are melancholy days.
there exist circumstances I put myself in, yet
always find someone else to blame.

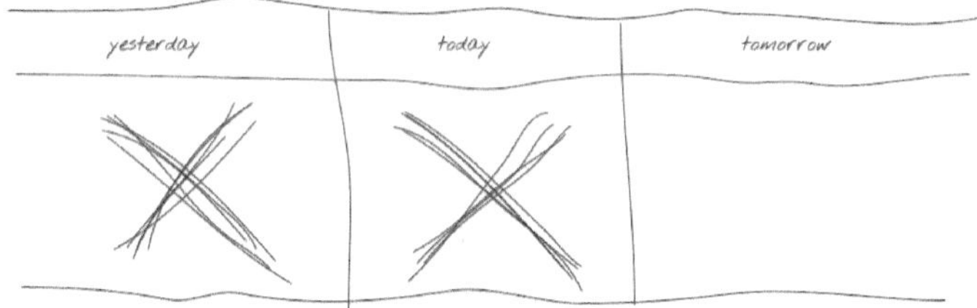

no, I will not pick up the phone;
because you open the faucet
and plug the drain; my mouth
flooding with saliva unstoppably;
I'm unable to hold back my
deepest depths, and they all
come pouring out in waves of
nausea through the wire; so
no, I will not pick up the phone.

when
I
must
be
silenced

I
am not.

when
I
need
to
speak

I
cannot.

August fades into September;
evaporating like water

the words drying up on my tongue
before I have the chance to speak them.

My mind speaks foreign tongues.
I cannot comprehend its howls;
Its snarls are inhuman; gutwrenching.
The beast scares me with its ceaselessness.
Raw meat satiates; bare paws on cracked,
Dusty Earth keeps the worst at bay.
Anything messy; animal; calms it for
Long enough to carve the good from bad.
I tape its mouth; punish; reprimand;
All before I remember that the beast is me.
And now I cannot scream for help.

what   now   ?

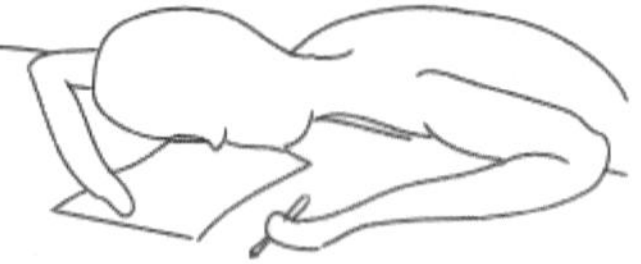

please

end.

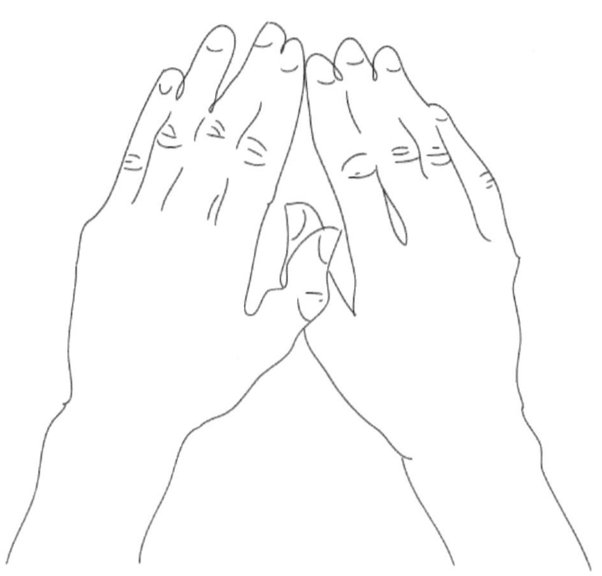

I. swallow me whole

II. mother's daughter

III. my fatal flaw

IV. grass and other blades

V. transcribe my mind

SHUT UP SHUT UP
SHUT UP SHUT UP SHUT UP SHUT UP
SHUT UP

do it again.

better.

I fear my fatal flaw is to speak.
but by now, it is
ten days too late and
ten fingers too many.
I have begun and I cannot stop;
a flow of delicate idiocies
illegible to all who aren't me.
my mind is untranscribable, thus
I rely on grass and other blades to heal.
swallowed whole and spit back out,
I am now certain that I am
plagued by the beautifully curated.
all this time, I have been my mother's daughter.

I.   'swallow me whole' immerses itself in the tangle of love and connection. It unravels the threads of affection, the shattering echoes of heartache, and the difficult task of holding emotional bonds. In its essence, it contemplates how the heart may beat with a fervor too strong for one's own good. Explore the author's intimate dance with both humanity and the world she calls home.

II.   'mother's daughter' delves into the realm of self-exploration. Within these pages, one navigates the odyssey of self-discovery, embraces the tender blossoms of self-acceptance, and nurtures the roots of personal evolution. The author touches upon the notion that our hearts cradle a wide variety of emotions, thoughts, and experiences that can be both a blessing and a burden.

III.   'my fatal flaw' is a voyage through life's treacherous sea of challenges. The verses mirror one's journey through the waves of adversity, showcasing the strength, fortitude, and unwavering spirit that propel one forward. Through ink-stained lines, the author explores the depths of our souls in order to find solace and inspiration in the delicacy between struggle and triumph.

cont.

IV.   'grass and other blades' walks itself through the whispers of grass and the myriad of blades beneath one's fingertips. Nature beckons, inviting a waltz of tactile revelation. An ode to sensory engagement, these pages unfurl the tapestry of human existence, weaving the narrative of how the intimate touch of nature both transforms and envelops us.

V.   'transcribe my mind' is animalistic and unapologetic. The author's writing forces the reader back into a prehistoric body of the unevolved human to better explore the depths of emotion. The metaphorical lens is adapted to discover various aspects of life and the human condition as the author pleads for a cognitive transcription.

about the author

Lauren Wander (she/her) is an 18-year-old from a suburb of the Twin Cities in Minnesota. Hobbies she currently enjoys are reading psychological thrillers, spending time with her loved ones, and scouring the cities for cool vintage clothes and good coffee. One of the standout qualities of Wander's poetry is its ability to resonate with readers on a deeply personal level. Through fictional poetry and prose, Wander uses her characters to capture the essence of the human experience; a creation nothing short of enchanting.

see also:
Seasons of Change *by Lauren Wander*

contact:
lwander24@gmail.com
https://linktr.ee/laurenwander
@wanderswriting on Instagram

ratings and reviews:
Honest reviews are highly appreciated and extremely helpful to the author. Please consider rating or reviewing work by Lauren Wander on any of the following:

BarnesandNoble.com / Amazon.com / Target.com / Walmart.com